A DIFFERENT WORLD

DEAFNESS

BY
ROBIN TWIDDY

KidHaven
PUBLISHING

Published in 2022 by
KidHaven Publishing, an Imprint of Greenhaven Publishing, LLC
353 3rd Avenue
Suite 255
New York, NY 10010

Edited by: John Wood
Designed by: Gareth Liddington

Cataloging-in-Publication Data

Names: Twiddy, Robin.
Title: Deafness / Robin Twiddy.
Description: New York : KidHaven Publishing, 2022. | Series: A different world | Includes glossary and index.
Identifiers: ISBN 9781534538405 (pbk.) | ISBN 9781534538429 (library bound) | ISBN 9781534538412 (6 pack) | ISBN 9781534538436 (ebook)
Subjects: LCSH: Deaf children--Juvenile literature. | Deafness--Juvenile literature.
Classification: LCC HV2392.T95 2022 | DDC 362.4'2--dc23

Printed in the United States of America

CPSIA compliance information: Batch #CSKH22: For further information contact Greenhaven Publishing LLC, New York, New York at 1-844-317-7404.

Please visit our website, www.greenhavenpublishing.com. For a free color catalog of all our high-quality books, call toll free 1-844-317-7404 or fax 1-844-317-7405.

Look out for these banners throughout the book to see how different people experience the world.

KEY:

Hearing impaired

Full hearing

This book was written and designed with accessibility for people with color vision deficiency and dyslexia in mind.

Photo credits:

Cover & Throughout – CkyBe, Serhii Bobyk, Evgenii Emelianov, paradesign, berkut, Great Vector Elements, Vector Up, 2&3 – Erica Smit, 4&5 – Andrey_Popov, Kalah_R, 6&7 – Africa Studio, Aaron Amat, Yurchanka Siarhei, 8&9 – 365_visuals, Erica Smit, 10&11– sondem Dragana Gordic, 12&13 – Claudio Divizia, 14&15 – fizkes, Littlekidmoment, 16&17 – Syda Productions, ChuangTzuDreaming, Fcikle, 18&19 – Anton27, Aquarius Studio, 20&21 – Andrey_Popov, TY Lim, 22&23 – Microgen, Rawpixel.com.

All facts, statistics, web addresses, and URLs in this book were verified as valid and accurate at time of writing.
No responsibility for any changes to external websites or references can be accepted by either the author or publisher.

CONTENTS

Words that look like this can be found in the glossary on page 24.

A DIFFERENT WORLD?

We all live in the same world, don't we? Well, for some people who have a <u>condition</u> known as deafness or hearing impairment, the world can seem a little different.

4

In this book you will have the chance to see what the world can be like for someone with deafness or hearing loss. It is important to understand how others <u>experience</u> the world and the challenges they face.

WHAT IS DEAFNESS?

People who are deaf have some type of hearing loss. This means they might have trouble hearing sounds that are quiet, loud, high, or low. Some people might not be able to hear at all.

Sound travels to our ears as waves. For many people, their ears pick up the sound waves and send a message to their brain.

Their brain then turns that message into sound.

7

Some people are born deaf, and some people become deaf later. People who are deaf do not get messages from their ears to their brains, so they do not know about the sounds in the world around them.

For some deaf people, there might be a problem with their ears that stops the sound waves from reaching inside. For others, the problem might be with how the messages reach the brain.

The doctor is checking to see if there is a problem inside the ear.

LIP READING

One of the main ways that people <u>communicate</u> is by speaking. Since deaf people cannot hear words, some deaf people learn how to lip read.

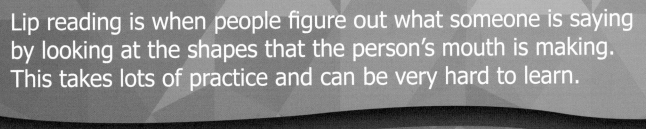

Lip reading is when people figure out what someone is saying by looking at the shapes that the person's mouth is making. This takes lots of practice and can be very hard to learn.

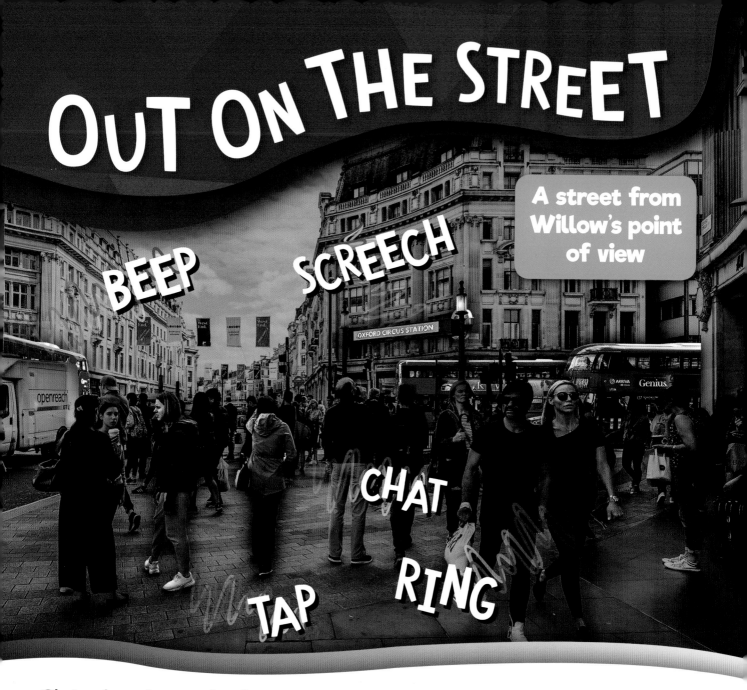

Out On The Street

A street from Willow's point of view

BEEP

SCREECH

CHAT

TAP

RING

Claire has been deaf since she was born, but her friend Willow can hear really well. Even though they are walking down the same street, they experience it a little differently.

Willow gets a lot of information about the world around her from sound. She can hear the cars, people, and animals around her. Claire doesn't hear everything, so she has to be <u>aware</u> in different ways.

Claire can't rely on her hearing; she needs to pay more attention to what she can see.

A street from Claire's point of view

SIGN LANGUAGE

There are lots of different sign languages, just like there are different spoken languages.

Deaf people use a type of language called sign language. It uses hand shapes, <u>facial expressions</u>, and body <u>postures</u> to make words and sentences.

Sign language is a great way to communicate. It is a really good idea to know some sign language even if you can hear. Then you can have conversations with sign language users.

This boy is using sign language. Can you make these signs?

Drink

Sorry

Thank you

MADE WITH DEAFNESS IN MIND

Vibration mode makes phone calls and text messages **accessible** to the deaf and hard of hearing.

There are lots of things that we own that use sound. Think about a smartphone – it makes noise when it receives a call, but it also has a vibration mode.

Some other cleverly made everyday objects that deaf people can use are:

Smoke alarms that vibrate and have flashing lights

Doorbells with lights

A product is deaf friendly if it tells us things using what we can see or feel, instead of hear.

GAMING WITH FRIENDS

Claire likes to play video games and so does her friend Willow. Willow plays games with a headset so she can talk to her teammates. Communicating can be really important in team games.

Claire plays games that use a keyboard. This means that she can type messages when she wants to talk to other players in the game. When Claire plays games, she turns on subtitles.

Subtitles are when the words spoken in a game, film, or TV show are written on the screen.

PARTIAL DEAFNESS

People with partial hearing might use a hearing aid. This makes sounds louder in their ear so they can hear better.

There are lots of types of deafness. Some people are completely deaf, but other people might have partial hearing loss. This just means that they have lost some of their ability to hear.

Some people use the terms mild, <u>moderate</u>, <u>severe</u>, and <u>profound</u> to say how bad their hearing loss is. People are more likely to lose their ability to hear high sounds such as women's or children's voices.

SUPPORT

There is a lot of help out there for people with hearing loss. People with partial or complete hearing loss can find help at school or at a doctor's office.

Even though people who are deaf like Claire may experience the world a little differently, we are more alike, all of us, than we are different.

GLOSSARY

accessible	being easily usable by people of different abilities
aware	being alert and taking notice
communicate	to pass information between two or more things
condition	an illness or other medical problem
experience	understanding of the world based upon the past and one's senses; sight, smell, hearing, taste, and touch
facial expressions	when the face is used to show emotions or thoughts, such as smiles or frowns
moderate	something that is not too strong or too weak
postures	the ways that a body is held
profound	an extreme level of something that affects other things
severe	serious, very great or intense

INDEX